Presenting Amazing Magnets

Teresa Celsi

Contents

Rigby

A Harcourt Achieve Imprint

www.Rigby.com
1-800-531-5015

Everyone enjoys a good show. Would you like to put on your very own play? You can make puppets to act out your play, just like real actors!

You can use magnets to make your puppet actors move. The magnets stay hidden underneath a stage you can make. Your audience will think the moving puppets are amazing!

You will need:

8½"×11" poster board

dark paint

large paper clips

tape (optional)

scissors

round magnets

paintbrush

**cereal box
(12 ounces or larger)**

craft sticks

glue

pencil and crayons

Make the Magnet Puppets

1. Bend part of a paper clip outward so that it looks like a T.

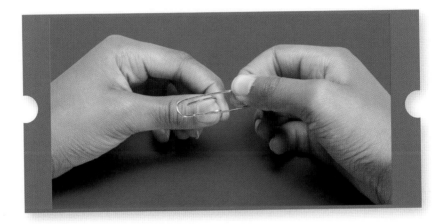

2. Place the paper clip flat on the table so that the bent part sticks up. This will be the puppet stand.

3. Fold a blank piece of poster board in half. Draw a puppet shape on one side.

4. Cut out your puppet through both parts of the poster board at the same time. Do not cut the area under the puppet's legs.

5. Color both sides of the puppet. Make it any character you want.

6. Glue the two insides of the puppet together, with the bent part of the paper clip between them.

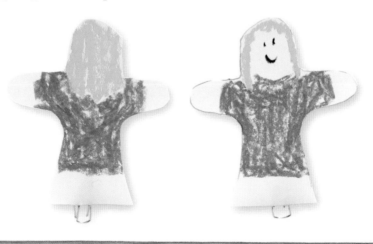

Now that you have made one puppet, you can repeat the steps to make as many puppets as you want.

Make the Stage

Now you can make a stage for your magnet puppets.

1. Cut out one of the long, thin sides of the cereal box.

2. Glue or tape the top of the box closed. You now have a box with one open side.

3. Set the box on a table with the back of the box facing down. Paint all the sides that you can see with dark paint.

4. Let the paint dry. Now you have a stage that you can reach under in the back.

5. Glue a magnet to the end of a craft stick. Hold the stick and magnet together for a minute. This will make sure that the magnet won't fall off.

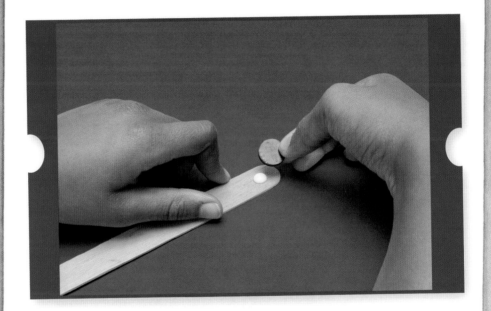

6. To complete the project, use poster board to make a back wall, just like a real theater. A back wall will keep the audience from seeing how you move the puppets.

Use the Puppet Theater

1. Place a puppet on your stage.

2. Hold the craft stick inside the box with the magnet facing up. When your stick moves near the paper clip, the puppet moves!

Now you can put on a puppet show without ever touching the puppets.

But how do the magnets work?

How Magnets Work

If you move your craft stick near the puppet, it will cling to the magnet. This is because the magnet attracts the metal in the paper clip.

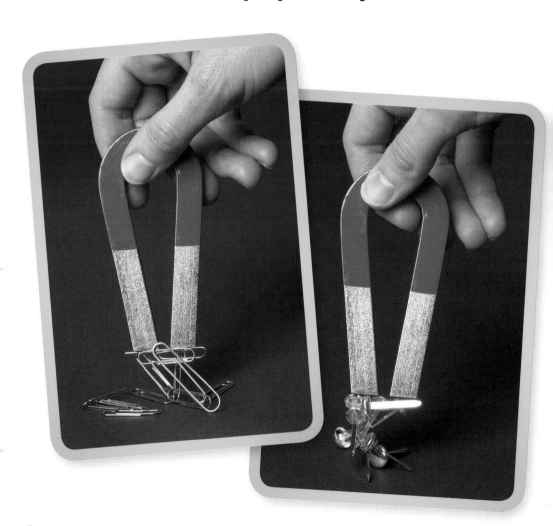

Magnets only attract certain metals. Steel and iron are easy for a magnet to attract. Magnets cannot attract copper or brass.

You cannot see a magnet's power, but you can see what it does.

Magnets do not work from very far away. A magnet must be close to a metal object to attract it. That is why you must hold the magnet right underneath your puppet to make it move.

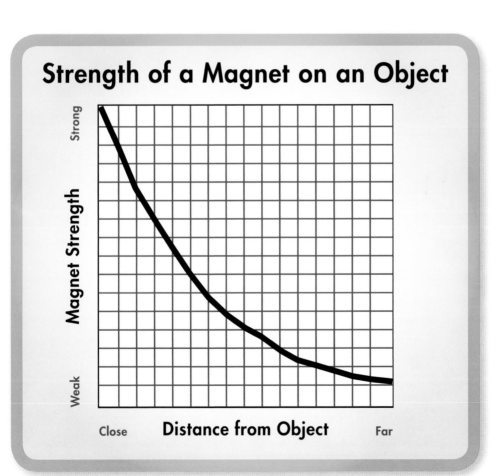

Strength of a Magnet on an Object

Magnet Strength

Strong

Weak

Distance from Object

Close

Far

Magnets All Around

Magnets help many people do their jobs. Huge magnets move metal junk.

Magnets also let people have fun. Televisions have magnets to help make a picture you can see.

Magnets are everywhere! You can use them in your science class.

You can use them at home to hang your artwork on the refrigerator.

Magnets are amazing tools. Now you know why magnets attract metal objects. You can use what you learned to entertain your friends!

Now Showing...

Myra's Merry Magnet Puppets

Index